WEEKLY WR READER
EARLY LEARNING LIBRARY

STATES OF MATTER
Solids

by Jim Mezzanotte

Reading consultant: Susan Nations, M.Ed., author/literacy coach/
consultant in literacy development
Science and curriculum consultant: Debra Voege, M.A., science
and math curriculum resource teacher

Please visit our web site at: www.garethstevens.com
For a free color catalog describing Weekly Reader® Early Learning Library's list
of high-quality books, call 1-877-445-5824 (USA) or 1-800-387-3178 (Canada).
Weekly Reader® Early Learning Library's fax: (414) 336-0164.

Library of Congress Cataloging-in-Publication Data

Mezzanotte, Jim.
  Solids / by Jim Mezzanotte.
    p. cm. — (States of matter)
  Includes bibliographical references and index.
  ISBN-10: 0-8368-6800-5 — ISBN-13: 978-0-8368-6800-5 (lib. bdg.)
  ISBN-10: 0-8368-6805-6 — ISBN-13: 978-0-8368-6805-0 (softcover)
  1. Solids—Juvenile literature. 2. Solid state physics—Juvenile literature.
  3. Matter—Properties—Juvenile literature. I. Title. II. Series.
  QC176.3.M49 2007
  530.4'1—dc22
                           2006010002

This edition first published in 2007 by
Weekly Reader® Early Learning Library
A Member of the WRC Media Family of Companies
330 West Olive Street, Suite 100
Milwaukee, WI 53212 USA

Editor: Gini Holland
Art direction: Tammy West
Cover design and page layout: Charlie Dahl
Picture research: Diane Laska-Swanke

Picture credits: Cover, title, © CORBIS; p. 5 © Mary Kate Denny/PhotoEdit; p. 7 (left) NASA/JPL-Caltech; pp. 7 (right), 11, 14 © David Young-Wolff/PhotoEdit; pp. 8, 13, 19 Melissa Valuch/© Weekly Reader Early Learning Library; p. 9 © Michael Newman/PhotoEdit; p. 10 © Bill Beatty/Visuals Unlimited; p. 15 © Larsh Bristol/Visuals Unlimited; p. 17 © Science VU/AMAX/Visuals Unlimited; p. 18 © G. Brad Lewis/Visuals Unlimited; p. 20 © Dennis MacDonald/PhotoEdit; p. 21 © Myrleen Ferguson Cate/PhotoEdit

Printed in the United States of America

1 2 3 4 5 6 7 8 9 10 09 08 07 06

Table of Contents

Cover and title page: Stonehenge is a famous landmark in England made of solid rocks. It was built hundreds of years ago.

Chapter One

A World Full of Solids

Solids are a form of matter. Do you know what matter is? It is all around you. It is anything that takes up space and has **weight**.

Mountains and oceans are matter. So is the air we breathe. Plants and animals are matter. People are, too. Almost everything in the universe is matter.

Matter can be in different forms, or states. It can be a **liquid** or a **gas**. It can also be a solid. Only solids hold their own shape. You can change a solid's shape, but it will not change on its own.

Solids make up most of our world. In school, your chair and desk are solids. Your books are solids, too. The clothes you wear are solids. So is the sandwich you eat at lunch. Do you see any other solids?

A classroom has many different solids.

Chapter Two

Properties of Solids

There are many kinds of solids. How can we describe them? The ways we describe them are called **properties**.

Solids can be different sizes. They can be huge, like the Moon. They can be tiny, like grains of sand. A **powder** is many tiny pieces of a solid.

Solids come in all sizes. The Moon is a huge solid. Grains of sand are tiny solids.

A solid has a weight. Two solids can be the same size, but they can have different weights.

metal spoon

plastic spoon

A metal spoon weighs more than a plastic spoon.

TRY THIS: Hold a plastic spoon in one hand. Hold a metal spoon in the other hand. Feel how the metal spoon is heavier than the plastic spoon.

Solids have different **textures**. Texture is how they feel. A solid can be smooth or rough. A marble is smooth. Sandpaper is rough.

A solid can also be hard or soft. Steel is very hard. Clay is soft. Wood is harder than clay but softer than steel.

These toys are solids. They have many different textures.

Some solids are very strong. Most bridges are made of steel, a strong metal. A steel bridge can hold many cars and trucks. Steel is heavy. Some strong solids are light. Spider webs are made of **silk** threads. They are light but very strong.

A spider's web is light but strong. Insects get caught in it and cannot escape. They become the spider's next meal!

Certain solids can be bent or stretched. They are **flexible**. You can bend a piece of wire. You can stretch a rubber band. Other solids do not change shape so easily. You cannot bend a rock!

What are some properties of a solid? It has a certain weight. It has a certain texture. The solid may be strong. It may also be flexible.

You can stretch a rubber band. It is a flexible solid.

Chapter Three

Mixed-Up Solids

Solids can be mixed together. Dirt is a **mixture** of solids. It is often dust, sand, rock, and dead plants.

Powdered sugar is a mixture of solids. It is a mixture of sugar and cornstarch.

A solid can mix with a liquid. Have you ever made chocolate milk? The cocoa powder is a solid. The milk is a liquid. When you pour the cocoa into the milk, it **dissolves**. The powder's tiny pieces spread out. They mix with the milk. A solution is a solid mixed with a liquid. Many solids mix with water.

chocolate powder

milk

dissolving chocolate powder

chocolate milk (solution)

Chocolate milk is a solution. It is a mixture of a solid and a liquid. The solid is cocoa powder. The liquid is milk.

This bowl of soup has solids on the bottom. They do not mix with the liquid.

Do you want to help a solid dissolve? Stir or shake the solution. Heat also helps a solid dissolve. But some solids and liquids do not mix at all. Some solid pieces may float. Other solid pieces just sink in the liquid.

Solids can also mix with gases. Oxygen is a gas in the air. Have you seen rust on a bike or car? The metal has mixed with oxygen and water to make rust.

A bike left in the rain will get rusty. The metal mixes with rain water and oxygen, which is a gas in the air.

Chapter Four

Changing Solids

A solid can change in many ways. Its shape can be changed. It can be bent or cut. Paper can bend. Paper can be cut. A solid can be crushed to make a powder. A solid can also burn. When it burns, some of it turns into ash.

Many solids melt if they get hot. They turn into liquids. When they cool down, they turn back into solids. A solid has a **melting point**. It is the temperature when the solid melts. Different solids have different melting points.

Liquid metal is poured into a mold. It will turn into a solid when it cools. The solid will have the shape of the mold.

Lava pours out of a volcano in Hawaii. When the lava cools, it will be hard rock.

Metal solids can turn into liquids. So can rocks. Some solids must get very hot to melt. When a volcano explodes, hot **lava** may pour out. Lava is liquid rock.

Solids can change the temperature of things close
to them. They **conduct**, or pass on, their heat or cold.
Heat from your hand makes an ice cube melt very
quickly. Cold from ice cubes can cool your drink.

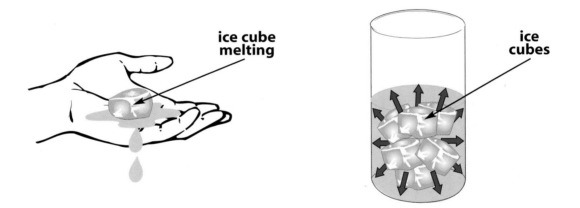

ice cube
melting

ice
cubes

Your hand passes heat to an ice cube, so it melts quickly.
But ice cubes can pass their cold to the liquid around them.

These carpenters are building a house. They use wood and other solids.

People often change solids. They cut trees into boards to make houses. They make tools, cars, and other things out of metal.

People use solids in many ways. Can you think of ways you use solids?

Clay is a solid. Using clay, you can make all kinds of things!

Glossary

conduct — pass on something, such as heat or electricity

dissolves — mixes in a liquid to create a solution

flexible — able to stretch or bend without breaking

gas — a form of matter. A gas cannot hold its own shape It expands to fill whatever is holding it, and it is not usually visible

lava — rock that erupts out of volcanos. It comes out as a very hot liquid, but then it cools and turns to a solid

liquid — a form of matter. A liquid cannot hold its own shape Instead, it takes the shape of whatever holds it

melting point — the high temperature a solid needs to reach to turn into a liquid

mixture — something that is made up of several things mixed together

powder — tiny pieces of a solid that has been crushed

properties — ways of describing something. Size and mass are two properties of a solid

silk — the strong, threadlike material of a spider's web. People use a different silk, from silk worms, to make clothes

textures — the ways something can feel when touched, such as smooth or rough

weight — measuring the force of gravity on an object

For More Information

Books

Everyday Physical Science Experiments with Liquids. Science Surprises (series). Amy French Merrill. (Powerkids Press)

Solids and Liquids. Young Discoverers: Science Facts and Experiments (series). David Glover. (Kingfisher)

Solids. Elementary Physics (series). Ben Morgan. (Blackbirch Press)

Web Sites

Science Clips: Solids and Liquids

www.bbc.co.uk/schools/scienceclips/ages/8_9/solid_liquids.shtml
This interactive site has many fun ways to learn about solids and liquids, for children of different ages.

Solids and Liquids

www.fossweb.com/modulesK-2/SolidsandLiquids
At this site, you can learn about how matter changes form.

Strange Matter

www.strangematterexhibit.com
Visit this site to learn about different kinds of solids.

Index

About the Author

Jim Mezzanotte has written many books for children.
He lives in Milwaukee with his wife and two sons.